CONTENTS

GIGA

Arranged by
CHRISTOPHER PARKENING

ROBERT de VISÉE

THE MYSTERIOUS BARRICADES

Arranged by
CHRISTOPHER PARKENING

FRANCOIS COUPERIN

Rondeau Vivament

Rondeau

GYMNOPEDIE No. I

Arranged by
CHRISTOPHER PARKENING

ERIK SATIE

Slowly and mournfully

GYMNOPEDIE No. II

Arranged by
JACK MARSHALL

ERIK SATIE

Slowly and sadly

GYMNOPEDIE No. III

Arranged by
CHRISTOPHER PARKENING

ERIK SATIE

THE GIRL WITH THE FLAXEN HAIR

Arranged by
JACK MARSHALL

CLAUDE DEBUSSY

*Diamond-shaped note indicates where to stop note with the left hand, while forefinger of right hand touches string at fret indicated.

CLAIR DE LUNE

Arranged by
JACK MARSHALL

CLAUDE DEBUSSY

THE LITTLE SHEPHERD

Transcribed by
JACK MARSHALL

CLAUDE DEBUSSY

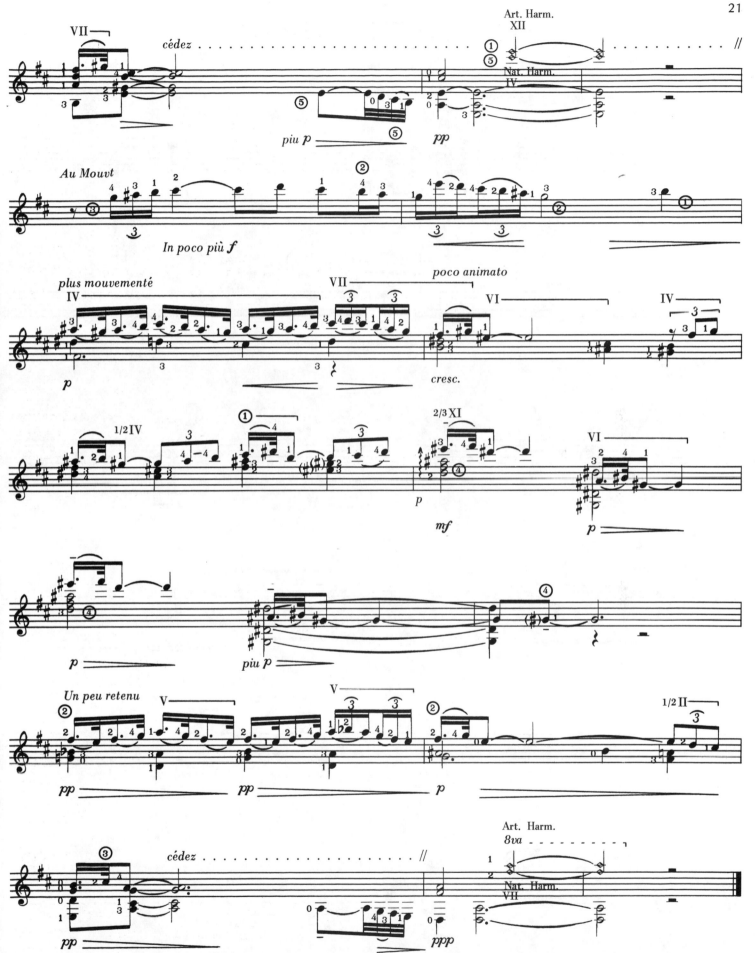

SARABANDE

Arranged by
CHRISTOPHER PARKENING

CLAUDE DEBUSSY